# THE CREATIVE WRITING PLAYBOOK

(For Kids ONLY!)

Megan Wagner Lloyd

Illustrated by Madeline Garcia

Andrews McMeel
PUBLISHING®

Andrews McMeel Publishing
a division of Andrews McMeel Universal
1130 Walnut Street, Kansas City, Missouri 64106

www.andrewsmcmeel.com

23 24 25 26 27 SDB 10 9 8 7 6 5 4 3 2 1

ISBN: 978-1-5248-7678-4

Made by:
RR Donnelley (Guangdong) Printing Solutions Company Ltd.
Address and location of manufacturer:
No. 2, Minzhu Road, Daning, Humen Town,
Dongguan City, Guangdong Province, China 523930
1st Printing – 1/9/23

Editor: Erinn Pascal
Art Director: Tiffany Meairs
Designer: Brittany Lee
Production Editor: Elizabeth A. Garcia
Production Manager: Chuck Harper

ATTENTION: SCHOOLS AND BUSINESSES
Andrews McMeel books are available at quantity discounts with bulk
purchase for educational, business, or sales promotional use. For
information, please e-mail the Andrews McMeel Publishing
Special Sales Department: sales@amuniversal.com.

**OOOH! CAN I BE A WRITER, TOO?**

Dear Kid Writers,

Do you dream of being an author when you grow up? Or maybe you like writing just for fun? Either way, I have good news for you. As a kid, you have a **super-awesome** skill that is actually really tricky for grown-ups: creativity! Just by being a kid, you are already a #1 expert at creativity. And just by being you and living in your unique and wonderful way, you have stories inside you that no one else could ever think of and that no one else could ever tell in just your way. That's right—you're a one-of-a-kind Creative Superstar, ready to shine bright. So go on, get those silly, scary, sweet, funny, zany, smart, **FANTABULOUS** ideas on the page! Let's get writing!

All my best,

Megan

Megan Wagner Lloyd, grown-up author

P.S. You can color and doodle on these pages, too!

This playbook
belongs to:

_____

_____

# PART ONE:

# HOW TO BUILD A STORY

# Planning a Story

You can plan a story by starting with three basic elements:

## #1: A Main Character

The star of your story!

Write one idea for a main character.

_____

_____

_____

_____

## #2: A Setting

Where your story takes place.

Write one idea for a setting.

_____

_____

_____

_____

_____

_____

_____

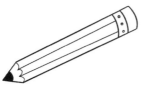

# #3: A Conflict

The problem that causes trouble for your main character.

Write one idea for a conflict.

_____

_____

_____

_____

_____

_____

_____

_____

_____

_____

_____

_____

_____

_____

# Introducing . . . Characters!

## Protagonist

A protagonist is the main character of your story. Usually, the protagonist actively makes choices that move the story along. Often the protagonist is also the hero of the story.

Draw a protagonist you'd like to write about.

I WONDER IF I'M . . . A CHARACTER!

## Antagonist

An antagonist is a character that works against a protagonist, bringing conflict to the story. Often, the antagonist is a villain and another main character in the story. (Not all stories have an antagonist. Sometimes the conflict comes from another source, like a natural disaster.)

Draw an antagonist you'd like to write about.

WAIT, WHAT IF I'M AN ANTAGONIST?

shiverrrr

# A Cast of Characters

Most stories have more than just a protagonist and an antagonist. They have a whole cast of characters. Think about each possible character and what they would bring to the story. Do they support the protagonist? Do they support the antagonist? Are they connected to the setting? Do they bring a sense of humor? A good example? A bad example? Will they change in the story (have a character arc) or stay the same?

Draw three ideas for characters.

# What's a Character Arc?

I WONDER IF I HAVE A CHARACTER ARC . . .

A character arc is the change that your character goes through from the beginning of the story to the end. Most, but not all, main characters have character arcs. Usually, some side characters have character arcs, too. (But some characters don't—they're the same at the beginning of the story and at the end.)

A character arc is the path a character travels as they interact with the conflicts, the setting, and the other characters.

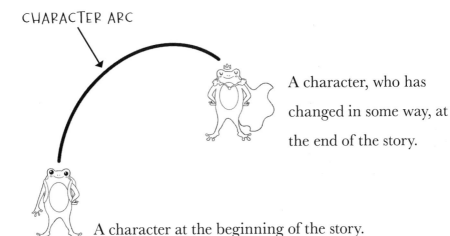

CHARACTER ARC

A character, who has changed in some way, at the end of the story.

A character at the beginning of the story.

# Make Your Own Character Arc

Start by brainstorming a main character. What is your character like at the beginning of your story?

_____

_____

_____

_____

What happens to your character during your story?

_____

_____

_____

_____

What's your character like at the end of your story? How have they changed?

_____

_____

_____

_____

# What's in a Name?

Things to think about when choosing character names:

- Do you want the name to fit their personality? Or **clash** with it?

- Do you want their name to reflect a specific culture, identity, or heritage? (Or more than one of the above!)

- Is your story set in our world or a made-up one? If it's an imaginary world, are the names similar to names somewhere on Earth or different?

- If your story is set in the past, look up what names were used during that time period.

- Do any of the names in your story sound similar in a way that might be confusing for readers? Consider switching up the beginning letters and the length and sounds in the names to help readers keep track of characters.

- Does your character like or dislike their name? Or do they not have a particular opinion about it?

# My Character Name Collection

Record your favorite character name ideas here!

# Fun with Names!

What funny names do you think would fit these characters?

———————   ———————   ———————

# Character Development Pages

Use these pages to expand on one of the characters you've been creating. (You'll get a few of these for tons of ideas!)

Name: _____

Age: _____

Hobby, Interest, or Job: _____

**Main Character** or *Side Character*

(Circle one)

**Protagonist** or *Antagonist* or Other

(Circle one)

What does this character want?

_____

_____

_____

_____

_____

What's stopping them from getting what they want? How do they respond?

_____

_____

_____

_____

_____

_____

_____

_____

Does this character have a character arc? If so, how have they changed by the end of the story?

_____

_____

_____

_____

_____

_____

_____

_____

_____

_____

# Character Development Pages

Use these pages to expand on one of the characters you've been creating. (You'll get a few of these for tons of ideas!)

Name: _____

Age: _____

Hobby, Interest, or Job: _____

**Main Character** or *Side Character*

(Circle one)

**Protagonist** or *Antagonist* or Other

(Circle one)

What does this character want?

_____

_____

_____

_____

_____

What's stopping them from getting what they want? How do they respond?

_____

_____

_____

_____

_____

_____

_____

Does this character have a character arc? If so, how have they changed by the end of the story?

_____

_____

_____

_____

_____

_____

_____

_____

_____

# Character Development Pages

Use these pages to expand on one of the characters you've been creating. (You'll get a few of these for tons of ideas!)

Name: _____

Age: _____

Hobby, Interest, or Job: _____

## Main Character or *Side Character*
(Circle one)

## Protagonist or *Antagonist* or Other
(Circle one)

What does this character want?

_____

_____

_____

_____

_____

What's stopping them from getting what they want? How do they respond?

_____

_____

_____

_____

_____

_____

_____

_____

Does this character have a character arc? If so, how have they changed by the end of the story?

_____

_____

_____

_____

_____

_____

_____

_____

_____

# Character
# Development Pages

Use these pages to expand on one of the characters you've been creating. (You'll get a few of these for tons of ideas!)

Name: _____

Age: _____

Hobby, Interest, or Job: _____

**Main Character** or *Side Character*

(Circle one)

**Protagonist** or *Antagonist* or Other

(Circle one)

What does this character want?

_____

_____

_____

_____

_____

What's stopping them from getting what they want? How do they respond?

_____

_____

_____

_____

_____

_____

_____

Does this character have a character arc? If so, how have they changed by the end of the story?

_____

_____

_____

_____

_____

_____

_____

_____

# Character Development Pages

Use these pages to expand on one of the characters you've been creating. (You'll get a few of these for tons of ideas!)

Name: _____

Age: _____

Hobby, Interest, or Job: _____

## Main Character or *Side Character*
(Circle one)

## Protagonist or *Antagonist* or Other
(Circle one)

What does this character want?

_____

_____

_____

_____

_____

What's stopping them from getting what they want? How do they respond?

_____

_____

_____

_____

_____

_____

_____

Does this character have a character arc? If so, how have they changed by the end of the story?

_____

_____

_____

_____

_____

_____

_____

_____

_____

# Six Settings

A setting is when and where your story takes place. Is your setting real? Or imaginary? Is it in the past, the present, or the future? How does the setting fit with the characters and the conflict? Brainstorm six settings you'd like to explore. They can be places you know in real life, places you've learned about through research, or totally made up!

1. _____

2. _____

3. _____

4. _____

5. _____

6. _____

# Picture This

Draw a picture of a place you'd like to explore in your writing.

# Design a Story Map

Have you ever read a book that has a map in it? Making a map of where your story takes place can help you plan the action of your story. Draw a map below, then trace the path your characters will take.

# Conflict vs. Conflict

You can choose from many types of conflict to develop your story. Conflicts don't have to be big or earth-shattering to be meaningful. What matters is that—big or small—they mean something to your main character. Some common conflicts include:

- a villain
- a natural disaster
- a new and challenging situation
- conflicting responsibilities
- conflicting loyalties
- hard-to-process emotions
- a manmade disaster
- change
- tiredness/physical distress
- lack of control
- conflicting goals
- an accident
- a misunderstanding
- mismatched personalities

What do you think is happening with these two characters?
Write about their conflict and how they can solve it.

_____

_____

_____

_____

_____

_____

# Planning a Plot Pyramid

One way to structure the plot of your story is by using a plot pyramid.

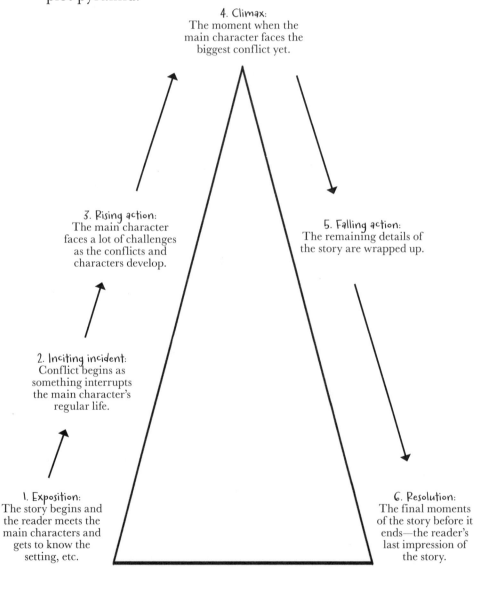

4. Climax:
The moment when the main character faces the biggest conflict yet.

3. Rising action:
The main character faces a lot of challenges as the conflicts and characters develop.

5. Falling action:
The remaining details of the story are wrapped up.

2. Inciting incident:
Conflict begins as something interrupts the main character's regular life.

1. Exposition:
The story begins and the reader meets the main characters and gets to know the setting, etc.

6. Resolution:
The final moments of the story before it ends—the reader's last impression of the story.

An example of a plot pyramid:

**Exposition**: The Creativity Creature and Cleo meet and become friends.

**Inciting incident**: They go on vacation to a desert island.

**Rising action**: They find a treasure map, look for treasure, fall into a trap . . .

**Climax**: And get totally lost! But, by working together, they find their way again . . .

**Falling action**: Step by step.

**Resolution**: And stay best friends—the best treasure of all!

# Plot Pyramid for My Story

Try planning a story using a plot pyramid.

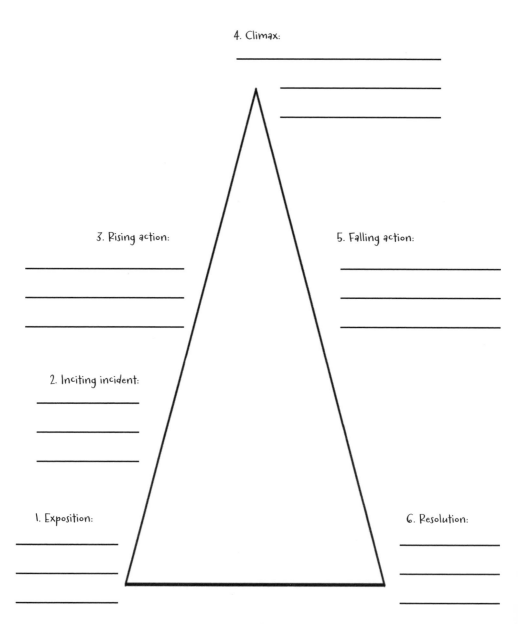

4. Climax:
_____
_____
_____

3. Rising action:
_____
_____
_____

5. Falling action:
_____
_____
_____

2. Inciting incident:
_____
_____
_____

1. Exposition:
_____
_____
_____

6. Resolution:
_____
_____
_____

# Story Starter: Secret Royalty

On the next few pages, use the story starters to come up with fun plots, and then add more to your stories on your own paper!

I never thought I could be a princess. How can a kid who's used to wiping runny noses, changing dirty diapers, and eating old oatmeal for every meal ever think they might be royalty? But that was before the sparkling gold carriage showed up and the queen stepped out and said . . .

_____

_____

_____

_____

_____

_____

_____

_____

_____

# Story Starter: UFO?

GRUMBLE . . . RUMBLE . . . _____'s eyes flew open. What was that sound? *Oof!* He tumbled out of bed. As he ran to the window, an eerie green light filled his room. _____ held his breath and watched as something, shining silver in the streetlight, landed below. It looked like . . .

_____

_____

_____

_____

_____

_____

_____

_____

_____

_____

_____

_____

_____

_____

# Story Starter: Ocean Adventure

"Whoo-hoo!" _____ cheered as she ran down the beach, splashing at the edge of the waves. The sand was warm, the sun beamed brightly overhead, and the water was just the right temperature for swimming. It was a perfect day. A perfect day, thought _____ , for finally figuring out what the rainbow-colored seashell she'd found could do. She already knew that it must be magic. _____ took out the shell and . . .

_____

_____

_____

_____

_____

_____

_____

_____

_____

_____

# Story Starter

_____

*(add your own title here)*

Write a story inspired by this picture.

_____

_____

_____

_____

_____

_____

_____

_____

_____

_____

_____

# Story Starter

_____

**(add your own title here)**

Write a story inspired by this picture.

BOO!

_____

_____

_____

_____

_____

_____

_____

_____

_____

_____

_____

_____

_____

# Story Starter

_____

*(add your own title here)*

Write a story inspired by this picture.

_____

_____

_____

_____

_____

_____

_____

_____

_____

_____

_____

_____

_____

_____

_____

_____

# Story Starter:
# Magic in the Park

_____ loved exploring the park. But he never expected to meet a magical creature there! It all started when _____ followed the flicker of a firefly down the trail, around the bend, behind a curtain of ivy . . . and into a hidden hollow. _____ gasped. He couldn't believe it was a real live . . .

_____

_____

_____

_____

_____

_____

_____

_____

_____

# Story Starter: The Haha Haunted House

*Creak!* The floor groaned as _____ crept down the stairs . . .

*Oooh* . . . the wind shrieked as _____ tiptoed down the hall.

*Eeeek* . . . went the door as _____ pushed it open . . .

And started laughing! *Hahahaha!*

Draw what＿＿＿＿＿＿ saw in the haunted house:

# Story Starter: The Case of the Missing Cookies

Detective _____ surveyed the scene. The cookie jar was broken. They inspected the floor with their magnifying glass. There was nothing left but—

"Crumbs," they said. "Crumbs that lead right to . . ."

What did the crumbs lead to?:

_____

_____

_____

_____

_____

_____

_____

_____

_____

_____

# The Storytelling Game

To practice making stories with main characters, settings, and conflicts, play this storytelling game.

## Directions:

Draw three main characters, three settings, and three conflicts in the boxes below.

| Characters | Settings | Conflicts |
|:---:|:---:|:---:|
| ↓ | ↓ | ↓ |

**Round One:** Write a story using the character, setting, and conflict in the first row.

_____

_____

_____

_____

_____

_____

_____

_____

_____

_____

_____

_____

_____

_____

_____

_____

_____

_____

**Round Two**: Write another story using the second row.

_____

_____

_____

_____

_____

_____

_____

_____

_____

_____

_____

_____

_____

_____

_____

_____

_____

_____

_____

_____

**Round Three:** Write another story using the third row.

_____

_____

_____

_____

_____

_____

_____

_____

_____

_____

_____

_____

_____

_____

_____

_____

_____

_____

_____

_____

**Round Four:** Next, try writing a story using a character, setting, and conflict each found on different rows.

———————————————————————————————

———————————————————————————————

———————————————————————————————

———————————————————————————————

———————————————————————————————

———————————————————————————————

———————————————————————————————

———————————————————————————————

———————————————————————————————

———————————————————————————————

———————————————————————————————

———————————————————————————————

———————————————————————————————

———————————————————————————————

———————————————————————————————

———————————————————————————————

Use extra paper to write stories with even more combinations of your characters, settings, and conflicts.

# Deciding How to Tell Your Story

You know you have a story to tell, but how do you want to tell it? What shape do you want your story to take? Think about what will suit your story best. You could even try telling the same story in more than one way to find the perfect fit.

Some of the possible shapes your writing can take:

# Writing

- a novel
- a poem
- a novel-in-verse (a novel where the story is told through poetry)

# Writing + Illustrations

- an illustrated novel
- a picture book
- a graphic novel
- a shorter comic

# Writing That Is Designed to Be Performed

- a play
- a screenplay
- a TV show or skit script
- song lyrics

# What Are Genres?

Genres are traditional categories that group different types of stories. You can write a story that fits in one genre. Or some genres can be combined (like writing a science fiction mystery!) Do you have a favorite of the genres below?

**Fantasy:** Stories with magic/supernatural elements

**Science Fiction:** Stories with advanced and/or imaginary scientific elements

**Mystery:** Stories focused on solving a puzzling/mysterious situation

**Memoir:** True stories from the writer's life

**Realistic Fiction:** Stories set in the real world, with realistic characters and problems

**Nonfiction:** Factual writing about true people, places, and events

**Historical Fiction**: Stories set in the real places and events of the past

**Horror**: Scary stories

# Fractured Fairy Tales

A fractured fairy tale is a fairy tale retold with a twist. See if you can retell one of the famous fairy tales below, but with your own special spin!

Start with a fairy tale, like:

⦾ "Little Red Riding Hood"
⦾ "Goldilocks and the Three Bears"
⦾ "Thumbelina"
⦾ "Hansel and Gretel"

And change one or more of the following:

## The Main Character

## How the Story Is Told

## The Setting

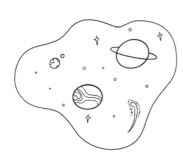 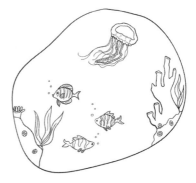

## The Ending

# Write Your Own Fractured Fairy Tale

The fairy tale you're starting with:

_____

_____

_____

_____

What you're changing in your retelling:

_____

_____

_____

_____

_____

_____

_____

_____

_____

_____

_____

# Point of View

You get to choose what Point of View (or POV) you want to use to tell a story.

## First person POV (Uses "I")

I ran into the monster's cave. "I'm not scared of monsters," I thought. But then the monster looked right at me! "AHHHH!" I screamed.

## Second person POV (Uses "You")

You ran into the monster's cave. You weren't scared of monsters. But then the monster looked right at you! "AHHHH!" you screamed.

# POV Practice, Part One

Write a few sentences from first person and second person point of view.

First person POV:

_____

_____

_____

_____

_____

_____

Second person POV:

_____

_____

_____

_____

_____

_____

_____

# Two More Points of View

**Third person limited POV (uses characters' names and can share the thoughts of the main character):**

The knight ran into the monster's cave. "I'm not scared of monsters," the knight thought. But then the monster looked right at her. "AHHH!" the knight screamed.

**Third person omniscient POV (uses characters' names and can share the thoughts of any character at any time):**

The knight ran into the monster's cave. "I'm not scared of monsters," the knight thought. Meanwhile, the monster had been dreaming of something tasty to eat. *Creak, clank!* "What was that?" wondered the monster. The monster opened its eyes. "A new friend!" it thought, meeting eyes with the trespasser. But the knight didn't understand that the monster wanted to be friends. "AHHH!" the knight screamed.

# POV Practice, Part Two

Third person limited POV:

_____

_____

_____

_____

_____

Third person omniscient POV:

_____

_____

_____

_____

_____

P.S. A quick summary of the rest of the story:

The knight soon learned that the so-called monster was actually very kind, and the knight and the monster became best friends and turned the cave into a very successful cupcake bakery! And everyone lived happily ever after.

# A+B+C

On the next page, write a story that includes: an adjective (descriptive word) from section A, a backdrop (setting) from section B, and a character from section C. Mix and match different combinations to **spark** new story ideas!

## A: Adjective

slimy ᴑ aqua ᴑ fluffy ᴑ stinky ᴑ spiky ᴑ curious ᴑ sharp ᴑ bubbly ᴑ brainy ᴑ creepy ᴑ elegant ᴑ lucky ᴑ sparkling

## B: Backdrop

volcano ᴑ video game ᴑ forest ᴑ haunted house ᴑ desert island ᴑ library ᴑ restaurant ᴑ zoo ᴑ cave ᴑ grocery store ᴑ skyscraper ᴑ outer space ᴑ beach

## C: Character

detective ᴑ magician ᴑ veterinarian ᴑ author ᴑ soccer star ᴑ unicorn ᴑ teddy bear ᴑ prince ᴑ aviator ᴑ artist ᴑ spy ᴑ singer ᴑ genius

The Creati

SHHH!

WE CAN DO THAT?! WRITE ON THE KID'S PAGES?

# Start with "What If?"

One great way to start a story is to ask yourself a "what if" question, like . . .

What if . . . my cat was an evil genius?

What if . . . I found a baby dragon?

What if . . . I could fly?

What if . . . I was given a magic wand?

What "what if" questions can you think of?

_____

_____

_____

WHAT IF . . . THE
CREATIVITY CREATURE
AND CLEO WERE IN
YOUR STORY?

# Write Your "What If?" Story

Look through the "what if" questions you've brainstormed. Pick your favorite question and use it as the inspiration for a new story!

_____

_____

_____

_____

_____

_____

_____

_____

_____

_____

_____

_____

_____

_____

# You're Invited . . .

Write a made-up invitation to a pretend party.

You're invited to a _____ party!

Where:

_____

_____

_____

_____

When:

_____

_____

_____

_____

# A Creativity Party

Write a story about what happens at the party. Who is invited? Who goes to it? Does it go well or are there party problems?

_____

_____

_____

_____

_____

_____

_____

_____

_____

_____

_____

# Fan Fiction

Fan fiction is creating stories or other art that is directly inspired by other authors' or creators' work. You can't take credit for these characters and worlds (since they are based on someone else's work), but they can still be fun to write and share with friends and other fans.

What if two of your favorite characters from books, movies, TV shows, or video games ended up living in the same fictional world?

Choose two favorite characters.

_____

_____

And decide which setting they'll meet in.

_____

_____

What problems would come up if these characters interacted in this setting? Choose a conflict.

_____

_____

_____

_____

And start your fan fiction story!

_____

_____

_____

_____

_____

_____

_____

_____

_____

_____

_____

_____

# An Ending Do-Over

Have you ever been really enjoying a book or movie . . . and then the ending just didn't work for you? Even when a story is well told, it's not always perfect for every kid.

Brainstorm what you would have done differently and why.

The title of the book or movie:

_____

_____

What was the story about?

_____

_____

_____

What did you love about this story?

_____

_____

_____

_____

_____

Why didn't you like ending?

_____

_____

_____

_____

_____

Rewrite the ending so that it's just right for you.

_____

_____

_____

_____

_____

_____

_____

_____

_____

_____

_____

_____

_____

# Creative Writing Prompts

You've already learned a lot about characters, setting, conflict, and guidelines for planning stories. But the truth is that, in creative writing, it's okay to **break the rules!** And it's okay to not have a plan. Sometimes it's fun to just write . . . for fun!

Without doing any planning beforehand, use these prompts as inspiration. Start here, and then use your own paper and see where your writing takes you!

1. You wake up in the most amazing house ever. Describe every room.

_____

_____

_____

_____

_____

_____

_____

2. Blast off! Your character is on their way to Mars. What happens next?

_____

_____

_____

_____

3. Your character has been given a dangerous secret spy mission to _____ . What's the mission? Do they succeed?

_____

_____

_____

_____

4. Your character makes a wish and it unexpectedly comes true! What happens next?

_____

_____

_____

_____

5. You've inherited a candy store! Describe it in detail, including the candy!

_____

_____

_____

# Make Your Own Writing Prompts

What ideas do YOU have? Write seven of your own prompts and use one a day for a whole week of creative writing fun.

1. _____
   _____
2. _____
   _____
3. _____
   _____
4. _____
   _____
5. _____
   _____
6. _____
   _____
7. _____
   _____
   _____

Start today! Choose one of your prompts, and write.

_____

_____

_____

_____

_____

_____

_____

_____

_____

_____

_____

_____

_____

_____

_____

_____

_____

_____

_____

_____

_____

_____

# Make a Mini Picture Book

Now that you have some ideas, you can use your own paper to make your very own picture book!

1. Get four pieces of paper and cut them in half, as shown.

Cut here! ⇒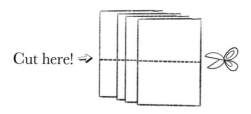

2. Next, stack the cut pages on top of one another.

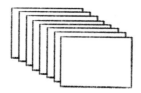

3. Then, fold all the pages in half, from left to right.

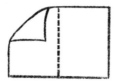

4. Now, your papers should be in this shape:

Folded end ⇒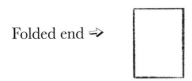

5. Last, staple twice at the folded end.

Staple ⇒

Staple ⇒

6. Now, it's time to write and illustrate your very own picture book!

# BLANK PAGE
So boring . . . hold on, you can change that! Doodle or write away!

# PART TWO:

# GETTING CREATIVE WITH COMICS!

# Comics Terminology

Comics are made of pictures and (usually) words. But what are the other parts of a comic called?

**SOUND EFFECTS** or **SFX** are onomatopoeia (page 106) that are often written directly in the art.

The **GUTTER** is the space between panels.

If there's a **NARRATIVE BOX** or **CAPTION**, it shares information about the time or place, or it tells more of the story.

Each box of bordered art is called a **PANEL**. A comic is usually made up of a sequence of panels.

# Making a Story with Writing and Art

Some stories are made up of just writing. Some stories are made of just art. But lots of stories have both writing and illustrations!

When you are making comics—or any other story with writing and art—try to make sure that the art and the words are adding different things to the story.

Here, the art and writing are sharing the same information:

The cat slept.

Here, the art and writing are sharing different information:

Casper dreamed of fish.

Draw a picture of a character.

Now, add a sentence about the character that shares new information that's NOT in the picture.

_____

_____

_____

# Draw a Four-Panel Comic Strip

**Panel 1:** Introduce a character.

**Panel 2:** Your character starts out on an adventure or is in a new situation.

**Panel 3:** Uh-oh, your character is in trouble!

**Panel 4:** Your character solves their problem in a surprising or funny way!

# Create Your Own Superhero

Not all comics have superheroes, but superhereoes are fun to create! Why not make one? Ask yourself these questions to help develop your superhero:

- Where did they get their superpowers?
- What special abilities do their superpowers give them?
- Does your superhero like having superpowers?
- What's one thing about their superpowers that makes their life easier?
- What's one thing about their superpowers that makes their life more difficult?

My superhero is named: _____

# Make a Comic Starring Your Superhero

**Panel 1:** Introduce your superhero.

**Panel 2:** Your superhero starts out on an adventure or is in a new situation.

**Panel 3**: Uh-oh, your superhero is in trouble!

**Panel 4**: Your superhero solves their problem in a surprising or funny way!

# Superhero Meets . . . Supervillain!

Make a comic starring your superhero (the protagonist) and a supervillain (the antagonist). How will your superhero defeat the supervillain and save the day?

# Story Starter: BFFs
# _____ and _____

Add the pictures and names to this comic:

_____ IS LONELY.

AND _____ IS BUSY. BUT _____ IS NEVER TOO BUSY TO . . .

SURPRISE, _____ !

BEST FRIENDS FOREVER, _____ AND _____ .

# Story Starter: Marigold's Giant Journey

Fill in the speech bubbles for this comic:

# DAY THREE

# DAY FOUR: THE END

# Story Starter: Robot's New Recipe

Finish this comic. What soup recipe does Robot invent?

Now, draw and write what happens next!

# Writing a Comic Script

One way to make comics is to start with a script. Scripts vary, but here's one way to write them.

## A S'mores Surprise! Script

**Panel 1:** A dragon sleeps next to a pile of beautifully wrapped presents.

NARRATION: It was Emerald's birthday.

SFX: Zzzz

**Panel 2:** Awake now, the dragon holds one of the presents, getting ready to open it, but a bit of the ribbon is tickling its nose.

EMERALD: Time to open my presents!

SFX: tickle

**Panel 3:** The dragon sneezes—in flames!

SFX: ACHOOO!

**Panel 4**: The dragon looks at the now burned presents.

EMERALD: Oops.

**Panel 5**: But one of the presents was marshmallows, which are now perfectly roasted!

EMERALD THOUGHT BUBBLE: Hmm . . .

**Panel 6**: Emerald enjoys s'mores for a surprise birthday treat!

EMERALD: Yum yum!

## A S'mores Surprise!

ZZZZ

TIME TO OPEN MY PRESENTS!

tickle

ACHOOO!

OOPS.

HMM . . .

YUM YUM!

Now it's your turn! Fill in this blank comic script:

## Panel 1:

NARRATION (optional): _____

_____

_____

(Character #1): _____

(Character #2): _____

SFX (optional): _____

## Panel 2:

NARRATION (optional): _____

_____

_____

(Character #1): _____

(Character #2): _____

SFX (optional): _____

## Panel 3:

NARRATION (optional): _____

_____

_____

(Character #1): _____

(Character #2): _____

SFX (optional): _____

# From Script . . . to Comic!

And turn your script into a three-panel comic:

Bonus activity! Ask a friend to read your script and illustrate it. How is their version the same as yours? How is it different? (Or you can illustrate your script again, but in a totally different way!)

# Comics Genre Challenge

You can use comics to tell all kinds of stories! Can you make a comic in one of these genres?

- Fantasy
- Realistic fiction
- Horror
- Memoir
- Science fiction
- Historical fiction
- Mystery
- Nonfiction

# Surprise Comics Shapes

Panels don't always have to be square or rectangles. They can be creative! Make a comic with these surprisingly shaped panels.

BLANK PAGE
. . . just waiting to be filled with fun!

# PART THREE:

# WOW! WHAT A WONDERFUL WORLD OF WORDS

# SMASH-ing Sound Effects

Including sound effects can make your story really **POP!** A word that sounds like its meaning is called an ONOMATOPEIA (now, that's a pretty cool-sounding word!). What sound effect words can you add to this list? **KAPOW!**

- buzz
- growl
- hiss
- burp
- swish
- vroom
- sizzle
- bark
- _____
- _____
- _____
- _____
- _____
- _____

- _____
- _____
- _____
- _____
- _____

SPLAT!

Make a comic filled with sound effects!

# Simile and Metaphor

SIMILE: Comparing two different things using "like" or "as."

> The dinosaur was as blue as a lake.
>
> The kid ran like a cheetah!

METAPHOR: Describing something by comparing two different things *without* using the words "like" or "as."

> Polly's eyes were stars.
>
> The basketball game was a rollercoaster.

# Write Your Own Similes

_____ was as _____ as _____

_____ is as _____ as _____

_____ was as _____ as _____

_____ is as _____ as _____

_____ was as _____ as _____

_____ is as _____ as _____

_____ like _____

_____ like _____

_____ like _____

# And Metaphors

_____ were _____

_____ was _____

_____ is _____

_____ were _____

_____ was _____

_____ is _____

_____ were _____

# Alliteration

ALLITERATION is grouping together words with the same beginning letters or sounds.

It can have different effects, depending on the sound you're repeating. It can make your writing:

Pop . . .

The pickiest purple pandas preferred pizza with peppers and pickles.

Or flow . . .

The seven sleek swans swam swiftly down the silent stream.

And more!

# Alphabetical Alliteration

Write alliterative descriptions repeating each of these letters:

T _____

_____

A _____

_____

D _____

_____

O _____

_____

W _____

_____

R _____

_____

C _____

_____

I _____

_____

L _____

_____

E _____

_____

N _____

_____

S _____

_____

# The Five Senses

Using the five senses in your writing can help readers feel like they're really experiencing your story. The five senses are sight, sound, smell, touch, and taste. Remember that not every writer—and not every character—uses all five senses or experiences them all in the same way. And that's part of what makes characters—and people!—interesting and unique. When writing, ask yourself what your characters are experiencing through the five senses.

Imagine a group of characters are having a special feast. What is it like?

## Sight
What does the food look like? What about the room? And the characters? _____

_____

_____

## Sound
Is there music playing? Are people talking? _____

_____

_____

## Smell

Does the meal have a smell? Are there any other smells in the room, good or bad? _____

_____

_____

_____

_____

## Touch

Is the food hot or cold? What type of silverware are they using? Or are they using their hands to eat? _____

_____

_____

_____

_____

## Taste

And what does the food taste like? _____

_____

_____

_____

_____

# A Favorite Feast

Using the sensory details you've brainstormed, write about this imaginary feast.

_____

_____

_____

_____

_____

_____

# The World through a Window

What can you see, hear, or smell from your window? Draw and write about what the view is like for you.

_____

_____

_____

_____

What if you were by a different window? Like the porthole of a boat? Or from way up high in a magic castle?

# Vivid Verbs

A verb is an action word—like "run," "dance," "talk," and "jump." There's nothing wrong with using familiar verbs in your writing. Sometimes that's what fits best! But other times using more descriptive verbs can be a way to add specific, vivid details to your story.

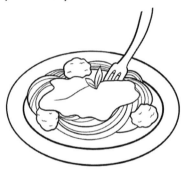

Mason ate the spaghetti. ⇨ Mason slurped the spaghetti.

Yuna ran around the corner. ⇨ Yuna careened around the corner.

Ahmad likes that poem. ⇨ Ahmad adores that poem.

I walked to the post office. ⇨ I dawdled to the post office.

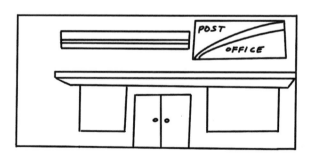

Write your own sentences with these vivid verbs:

Zapped: _____

_____

_____

_____

Grumbles: _____

_____

_____

_____

Snuggled: _____

_____

_____

_____

Dashed: _____

_____

_____

_____

# Writing Dialogue

DIALOGUE is when characters speak to one another. In writing, dialogue is shown by using quotation marks, like this: "Hello!" In comics, dialogue is shown in speech bubbles, like this:

Try these tips for writing better dialogue:

- Pay attention to the conversations around you. How do people change the way they talk when they are telling a story? In a hurry? Discouraged? Happy?
- Does the dialogue reflect the way the character is feeling in that moment?
- Read your dialogue out loud. Do you like the way it sounds? Or do you think it could be trimmed or reworded?
- Compare the speech of your different characters. Is the dialogue showcasing their different personalities?

# Dialogue Duo

Write two characters' conversation in the speech bubbles!

Character's
Name

Character's
Name

# A Super-Silly, Simply Splendiferous Word Collection

Some words are just fun to read and especially to say out loud! All of these are real words . . . but they also sound like made-up magical creatures! Circle your favorite-sounding one and draw what a creature with that name might look like.

snollygoster

hullabaloo

whippersnapper

flabbergast

scalawag

mollycoddle

skedaddle

whirligig

hogwash

argle-bargle

brouhaha

collywobbles

flibbertigibbet

Make up your very own fun-to-say word.

_____

What does your word mean?

_____

_____

_____

Now it's your turn to be a Word Collector! Record your favorite silly, magical, dreamy, funny, peppy, unusual, and simply fun-to-say-out-loud words!

| | |
|---|---|
| | |
| | |
| | |
| | |
| | |

# BLANK PAGE
## (But not for long!)

# PART FOUR:

# YOU ARE A STORYTELLER

# Finding the Stories in YOU

Sometimes, writers get ideas for their stories from their real-life experiences. Even fantasy authors, who make up a lot of magical elements for their books, still draw from their lives for ideas.

**Fact #1**: No one is exactly the same as you, and no one is living exactly the same life you're living.

**Fact #2**: Writers get ideas for characters, settings, and stories from their personalities, lives, and experiences.

**Fact #3**: So, no one can tell exactly the same stories you can tell! In other words, you have super-unique stories just waiting for you—and ONLY you—to write them!

NOW THOSE ARE SOME FANTASTIC FACTS!

# Brainstorming
## _____'s Stories

(write your name here)

Some of the things I love are . . . _____

_____

_____

_____

Some unique or unusual experiences I've had are . . . _____

_____

_____

_____

Some of my favorite memories are . . . _____

_____

_____

_____

Some people who are important to me are . . . _____

_____

_____

_____

_____

# Your Creativity Is a Treasure, and YOU Are, Too!

Fill the heart with things you like about yourself. How many kind things can you say about YOU?

# A Heart Hug

Fill the heart with things you like and appreciate about a family member or friend. Then show it to them or take a picture of it to share with them!

# An Acrostic Poem
# Starring You!

In an acrostic poem, the first letter of each word or line forms another word vertically, like this:

BIRDS

Blue

Iridescent

Roosting

Downy

Soaring

Write an acrostic poem where your name fills the vertical line and then choose words that match each letter to describe yourself.

128

# Dear Diary

Recording your day-to-day experiences in a diary can give you ideas for your stories. Plus, it's fun! Try to write every day for a week and see if you like it!

## Monday
Dear Diary, _____

_____

_____

_____

_____

## Tuesday
Dear Diary, _____

_____

_____

_____

_____

## Wednesday
Dear Diary, _____

_____

_____

_____

## Thursday

Dear Diary, _____

_____

_____

_____

_____

## Friday

Dear Diary, _____

_____

_____

_____

_____

## Saturday

Dear Diary, _____

_____

_____

_____

_____

## Sunday

Dear Diary, _____

_____

_____

_____

# Write a Fictional Diary

What if your character wrote a diary? What would they write about each day? Did you know you can write a whole book that is just diary entries or letters or emails or texts? It's called an **EPISTOLARY NOVEL**. Start your character's diary below!

Dear Diary, _____

_____

_____

_____

_____

_____

_____

_____

_____

_____

_____

# Nature Journaling

Next time you're outside, pay attention to the natural world. What's the weather like? Do you see any animals? What's growing, big and small? What else do you notice around you?

Recording your nature observations can help inspire your settings and bring vibrant details to your writing. Fill this page and the next with your nature drawings and notes!

# Be a Pretend Pen Pal

Being a pen pal is a great way to practice your writing. But what if you could write to characters? What would you tell them about yourself? What would you ask? Write a letter to a fictional character.

Dear _____ ,
(character's name)

_____

_____

_____

_____

_____

_____

_____

_____

_____

_____

From _____

(your name)

What if your pretend pen pal wrote back? How would they answer your questions? What questions would they have for you? Write their letter back to you, too.

Dear _____ ,

(your name)

_____

_____

_____

_____

_____

_____

_____

_____

_____

_____

_____

_____

_____

From _____

(character's name)

# Write from Your (Silly) Heart!

When you're not busy writing, what do you like to do? What do you love to learn about? What makes your heart sing? Make a list of four things you LOVE.

1. _____

_____

_____

2. _____

_____

_____

3. _____

_____

_____

4. _____

_____

_____

Next, finish this list of four silly and imaginative things.

1. The tallest sandwich in the world

2. An underwater tree house

3. _____

4. _____

Now, write a story that mentions all four things you love AND all four silly things!

_____

_____

_____

_____

_____

_____

_____

_____

_____

_____

_____

# A Friend's Favorites

The things you love can inspire your writing. But all of your characters won't be exactly like you! Interview a friend or family member to learn about another perspective.

_____'s Favorite . . .

1. Food: _____

2. Place: _____

3. Holiday: _____

4. Animal: _____

5. Color: _____

## My Friend

# A Character's Favorites

To create a character's favorite things, choose some of your favorite things AND some of the favorites from the person you interviewed.

My Character's Favorite . . .

1. Food: _____

2. Place: _____

3. Holiday: _____

4. Animal: _____

5. Color: _____

Draw a picture that includes all five favorites in it!

# Practicing Creativity

"You can't use up creativity.
The more you use, the more you have."
—Maya Angelou

When you hear the word "practice," you might think of practicing piano scales or going to soccer practice. Just like you can improve at piano and soccer—and writing!—by practicing, you can also become more creative by practicing creativity. Try these ideas for boosting your creativity!

- Make and decorate an important building (or even an entire town!) from your story out of recycled containers or modeling clay.
- Draw your characters. What do they look like? What do they wear? Bonus activity: make paper dolls or sculptures of your characters!
- Get out of your comfort zone by writing something really different than what you usually write.
- With an adult's help, cook or bake something from the world of your story.

- Record a book trailer for your story.
- Brainstorm one new story idea every day for a week, and then write your favorite idea.
- What books would your character read? Make a mini version of their favorite book.
- Draw a wordless comic or picture book.

Add two more creative ideas for practicing creativity!

- _____
- _____

# Your Writing Can Be a Gift

You can use your writing to lift others. Write a poem for a friend or family member and read it to them!

To: _____

_____

_____

_____

_____

_____

_____

_____

_____

_____

_____

_____

_____

From: _____

# A Gift for You, Too

Write a poem just for you. (Shhh! You don't have to let anyone else read it.)

_____

_____

_____

_____

_____

_____

_____

_____

_____

_____

_____

_____

_____

_____

_____

# Learning Storytelling

You're writing and writing and writing some more. What else can you do to learn about writing and storytelling?

## ENJOY THE THEATER

Go see a play . . . or even be IN a play!

## MAKE MOVIE MAGIC

Make your own mini movies.

After watching a movie, write a review! What did you like? What did you LOVE? What would you change?

## READ!

See the next page for a BIG reading challenge!

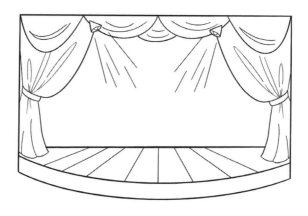

# The BIG Reading Challenge

Can you read a book in every one of these genres and storytelling styles? Color in each book as you read it! Add your own drawings of books you've read until all three shelves are full.

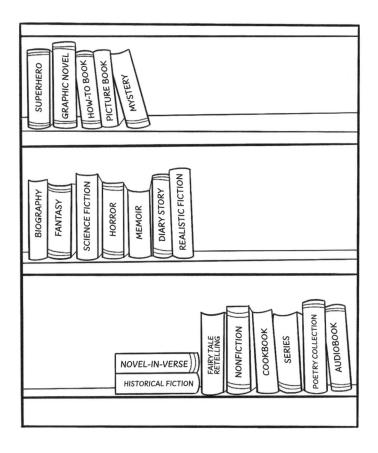

Not every genre will be your favorite. But it's always interesting to try new things. And if you read a book from a genre you don't end up liking, then perhaps be a bit like the Creativity Creature . . .

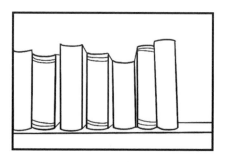

# Building Writing Habits

Remember: no two people are exactly the same. That means no two writers are exactly the same. What works for one writer might not work for another. What's important is that you find the writing habits that work best for YOU.

Try these ideas for building strong writing habits!

- Figure out what time of day you find it easiest to focus: Morning? Evening? Afternoon?
- Dedicate a special notebook for writing.
- Carry a small notebook with you so you can jot down ideas, observations, poems, and sketches on the go.
- See if one of your friends or family members wants to be writing buddies.
- Try different goal-setting techniques to learn what you prefer. Do you like to write daily or weekly or every other day? Do you like to time yourself as you write? What about trying to fill a certain number of pages or write a certain number of words?
- Experiment to see if you like working better in a quiet or chatty place.

# The Writing Rhythm

Try making a music playlist to listen to while you write. Some writers listen to music as background noise to stay focused. Others make playlists based on the mood of the chapter or book they are working on.

What songs would you put on these playlists?

## Focused Work

- ○
- ○
- ○
- ○
- ○
- ○

## Dramatic Fight

- ○
- ○
- ○
- ○
- ○
- ○

## Magical Moment

- ○
- ○
- ○
- ○

## Disaster Zone

- ○
- ○
- ○
- ○

## Training Time

- ○
- ○
- ○
- ○

# Questions for Revision

You've poured your heart and hard work into a story. But when you go back and read it again, you can tell it needs improvement. But what should you change? And how?! Revising can be intimidating! If you have a friend or family member who likes to write, try swapping stories and sharing feedback. If you're rereading your work on your own, try asking yourself these questions to get started with revision:

- Do the events in the story make sense? Do I need to add any additional scenes or explanations?
- Does my main character have a character arc?
- When I read the dialogue out loud, does it sound natural?
- Were any parts boring to read again? What can I add to the setting, the action, or the characters to make them more interesting?
- Have I used the senses in my descriptions?
- Are there any parts I can cut without losing anything important to the story?
- What are the best parts? What can I do to make the other parts shine as brightly?

- Does my beginning make me want to read more? And does my ending feel like the story stopped at the right place?
- If my story has illustrations, are the art and writing repeating each other or showing different aspects of the story?

Use the space below to ask questions or brainstorm answers for your revision.

_____

_____

_____

_____

_____

_____

_____

_____

_____

_____

_____

_____

_____

# My Revision Plan

My favorite thing about my story:

_____

_____

_____

_____

_____

What else I like about my story:

_____

_____

_____

_____

_____

What I want to change to make it even better:

_____

_____

_____

_____

_____

# The Power of Persistence!

You wrote something. You revised it. But wait . . . it still isn't perfect?! OH NO!

Take a deep breath. And remember: no one is perfect. And no one's writing is perfect. But that doesn't mean that you can't keep writing for fun, or that you can't keep learning and improving your writing, or that you can't keep telling stories.

Try to remember the power of persistence. "Persistence" means working very hard at something even when it's challenging.

Even when your writing doesn't turn out exactly right and even when you realize it needs more changes again . . .

You can't be perfect, but you can be persistent!

# The Fabulousness of FUN!

But writing isn't just about persistence. It's also about HAVING A BLAST! Jot down FIVE story ideas that sound extra FUN to write:

1. _____

_____

2. _____

_____

3. _____

_____

4. _____

_____

5. _____

_____

Choose the idea that sounds like the most **SUPER-DUPER** fun of all . . . and write it!

_____

_____

_____

_____

_____

# My Fabulous Fun Story

_____

_____

_____

_____

_____

_____

_____

_____

_____

_____

_____

_____

_____

_____

_____

_____

_____

_____

_____

_____

_____

_____

_____

_____

_____

_____

_____

_____

_____

_____

_____

_____

_____

_____

_____

_____

_____

_____

_____

_____

_____

_____

_____

_____

_____

_____

_____

_____

_____

_____

_____

_____

_____

_____

_____

_____

_____

_____

_____

_____

_____

_____

_____

_____

_____

# Books by You

Fill in the titles and design the covers for four books you'd like to write someday!

By _____

By _____

By _____

By _____

# The End

# Bonus
# Creative Writing BINGO

Complete and cross off five creative writing activities in a row to get Bingo. . . . Or for an extra challenge, do every single activity, including adding your own creative writing challenge in the last square!

## B I N G O

| B | I | N | G | O |
|---|---|---|---|---|
| Set a timer and write for thirty minutes. | Make a comic starring your favorite animal. | Describe the room you're in. | Write (and send!) a letter or postcard. | Write about two characters who are opposites. |
| Write a poem about a nonfiction topic. | Write a story starring one of your toys or collectibles. | Write a mystery starring a kid detective. | Write about one of your favorite memories. | Make a comic about a day in your life. |
| Write five days in a row. | You found a secret message. What does it say? | FREE SPACE | Set a timer and write for forty-five minutes. | Make a comic from the villain's POV. |
| Write about your favorite day of the year. | Write a story starring a friend or relative. | Write a story in which the characters travel back in time. | Make a fractured fairy tale picture book. | Set a timer and write for one hour. |
| Make a comic set in outer space. | Write a song. | Create a magical character for a fantasy story. | Write a story starring The Creativity Creature and Cleo. | |

Use the next pages to record story ideas and take notes!

_____

_____

_____

_____

_____

_____

_____

_____

_____

_____

_____

_____

_____

_____

_____

_____

_____

_____

_____

_____

_____

_____

_____

_____

_____

_____

_____

_____

_____

_____

_____

_____

_____

_____

_____

_____

_____

_____

_____

_____

_____

_____

_____

_____

_____

_____

_____

_____

_____

_____

_____

_____

_____

_____

_____

_____

_____

_____

_____

_____

_____

_____

_____

_____

_____

_____

_____

_____

_____

_____

_____

_____

_____

_____

_____

_____

_____

_____

_____

_____

_____

_____

_____

_____

_____

_____

_____

_____

_____

_____

_____

_____

_____

_____

_____

_____

_____

_____

_____

_____

_____

_____

_____

_____

_____

_____

_____

_____

_____

_____

_____

_____

_____

_____

_____

_____

_____

_____

_____

_____

_____

_____

_____

_____

_____

_____

_____

_____

_____

_____

_____

_____

_____

_____

_____

_____

_____

_____

_____

_____

_____

_____

_____

_____

_____

_____

_____

_____

# (Now It's Really)
# The End